Quit Your Day Job

Escape the Great American Hoax and Live Free

By

Oliver Trojahn

Dedication Page:

This book is dedicated to Robert Kiyosaki and Tim Ferriss, two of my favorite mentors. It is impossible to put into words how much their knowledge has transformed my entire life, beliefs, and mindset.

Reading books is a requirement for success in this world and reading the right book at the right time is even more critical. Their books came into my life three years ago at the RIGHT TIME and I will forever be grateful.

I have read over 200 books in the last three years, and these two authors are at the top of my list. If you haven't already, I highly recommend that you read the following two books, because, of the 200 that I have read, they are my top two favorites:

Retire Young, Retire Rich by Robert Kiyosaki

The 4-Hour Workweek by Tim Ferriss

Contents

Introduction

The Great American Hoax

You've been taught something specific your entire life. Your parents taught you when they gave you an allowance to do your chores. Your teachers taught you when they graded your schoolwork. That job you had selling popcorn at the movies taught you. College taught you. Your first real job taught you.

You were taught to believe in the American Dream.

We are told that there's one way to succeed in life. Go to school. Get the degree. Get the job. Get promoted. Then you buy the house, start the family. You work hard enough, and you lock this down by your early twenties. Afterward, you can look forward to enjoying the good life.

This is the American Dream. It's the idea that you can lead the good life by going to the best college, getting good grades, landing the great job, and once you do that, you can settle down. You've got a job for life. You've paid out a huge down payment on a nice house. You'll get married. Start a family, and then it's easy street.

At least that was my experience of the American Dream. I got my degree. I got married and bought a house. I actually bought a house before I even started my job, and the job was going to pay for all of it. It was going to be the focus of my whole life.

My entire life was directed toward getting that job. It was about excelling at everything I did to be successful and make the most money. I graduated college with the house and job lined up. I was twenty-four years old. I was about to get married. Everything was on course.

I had it better than most. People would give their kidney for what I had set up coming out of college. I had worked very hard to get there because it was all I knew, and I did it all perfectly.

But I didn't know there were other ways to do it.

I didn't know that my American Dream was slowly turning into a real nightmare.

Things didn't work out the way I'd expected. It wasn't like they said it was going to be.

First, my marriage fell apart. We were too young, and it soon became apparent that we wanted different things out of life, which got me to question what the American Dream was all about. The American Dream tells you that once you get married and settle down that's it. It encourages people to get married too early—right out of college when you might not even have met the girl of your dreams.

I got divorced because I knew there was something more to life. It wasn't just about settling down and living the life you're supposed to live. There was something more out there, and I was hungry for it. I had the job and the wife, just like all my friends. Then they started having children, and we thought about having them, too, but I realized that if it carried on like this, I would just be doing the same thing as all my friends, and we'd all be just like each other. It's crazy to think that you're losing the part of yourself that makes you unique.

At the same time, I was losing faith in my corporate job. It looked fine from the outside. I thought I was making good money. I could count on a healthy bonus. I was doing the work and putting in the hours. I was doing everything you have to do to scale the corporate ladder.

But it was too much and also not enough. Too much time for too little reward. Too much of my life was slipping away working nights, while my paycheck never seemed to keep up with how I valued my time.

I started looking for other opportunities. I started investing in real estate, and before long, I started to see that there were better ways to make a living than killing yourself in a corporate job.

The problem wasn't about going to college. Education is incredibly important, and I think that most people will greatly benefit from a college education. The problem wasn't even having that first job. It taught me a lot about the corporate world and how big organizations operate.

The truth is, however, that you have to start doing other things or you won't be able to retire. You have to break out or you'll be just like everybody else. Some people are okay with that. I was not, and if you're reading this book, I know that you are not okay with that either.

Imagine three people that you know. One makes $75,000 a year. One makes $150,000. Another makes $300,000. Most people would get real excited to make as much money as the second or third person. They think that's what it takes to make it, to feel secure.

I can tell you right now, though, that they are all the same person. One will have a slightly nicer car or a slightly bigger house, but their cash flow is exactly the same because of taxes. They're working the same grind, and they're no different.

Can you imagine making $400,000 a year? People dream of a salary like that, but are you any better off? You have a slightly better house and car, but those aren't going to make your life better in any way. They won't make you unique. You're just more of a slave to the corporate job. Your cash flow is basically the same as someone making much less. After you take taxes into consideration, you'd be better off making $75,000 a year. You'll have a slightly worse house and a slightly less impressive car, but no one cares about that anyway.

So, what's the alternative? What choice is there besides playing the corporate game and striving for that slightly superior car?

Let's say there's a fourth person who makes only $50,000 a year, less than any of these other people, but he puts his money into real estate. He's getting a feel for the market, but he's also getting a feel for what financial freedom could look like. The money he makes off each house he acquires could be chump change. It could be just another $5,000 a year cash flow on the side, but it starts to add up. He starts to realize that he doesn't need a paycheck. He's opening up to a whole new way of doing things.

You can absolutely make $5,000 a year by buying a $100,000 house and renting it out. I know because that's how I got started in real estate, but that $5,000 you make on rentals is tax free. So it's actually the equivalent of making $10,000 in a corporate job. That's the real game changer.

The real difference, however, is power and freedom. Someone making $50,000 a year with some real estate investments on the side is going to be more powerful than the CEO of his company. The CEO works thirty years of his life to pull in a multimillion-dollar salary. That's nothing to sneeze at, but he had to work thirty years to get it. What'd he do for thirty years? He was grinding and slaving away his whole life. Working nights. Weekends. No time to do what he wants to do. No time to spend with his family. Just doing whatever other people tell him to do to get his chance at the big times.

You could make only $20,000 a year and be more powerful than the CEO of your company if you're investing in real estate on the side, starting online companies, or doing something that will make you real money. You'll certainly be more powerful than the people doing the same job for $75K, $150K, or even $400K.

This is why the American Dream is actually the American Hoax. College doesn't teach you why the 1% is getting richer and richer, while wages are stagnant for everyone else. Your parents don't tell you that you can retire at thirty and live off real estate rentals as I did. There are so many better ways to make money. In the Information Age and with online sales, anyone can make money in real estate or by starting their own company. You don't need to have the greatest idea or the next best thing. All you need to do is start. With the number of people on the Internet now, it's never been easier to make a ton of money quickly.

They don't teach you how money is really made in America. The real way to make money is real estate investment and business ownership because of the way our taxes are structured. You pay almost nothing in taxes when you invest in real estate. Leveraging tax advantages is the surest way to make massive amounts of money and free up your time for more important things.

The reality is that a corporate job will never make you money. A job will just make your life like everybody else's. You won't have real money. You won't really change the world. You'll be just like everybody else.

If you want more, you have to do other things. You have to start investing in real estate. You could start your own business or company, but you can't just depend on your corporate job.

We see proof of the American Hoax all around us. The hollowing of the middle class. People with jobs that are great on paper still struggling to get by. I know people in New York who make half a million dollars a year on Wall Street and still living paycheck to paycheck. It happens all the time. Their house is a little bigger, and they've got a slightly better car, but their lives are exactly the same as people making much less, and they don't understand that they'd be happier and better off getting out of the game entirely.

People think that investing in real estate or starting your own company is risky. They're wrong. Doing those things makes your life less risky. The real risk is spending your whole life just getting by. Look at the destruction of the middle class. All these people who believed they'd be taken care of if they worked hard and stuck with their corporate jobs. How's that working out for parents who can't afford their children's college tuition, or people who can't afford to retire?

Why do you think the 1% keeps getting richer? It's not magic. They're not better than everybody else, but they have the skills and ideas that you need to succeed in today's economy, and these are the skills and ideas that will be presented in this book.

I quit my corporate job, and now I'm part of the 1%. It took me a few years to get here, but it was much quicker than if I'd kept trying to climb the ladder. Most of all, you would not believe how much money I make while putting in the least number of hours.

If you want to retire from working a corporate job, it's going to take you forty years. That's 98,000 hours. By investing in real estate, I've made enough to retire in five years or about 800 hours. Are you kidding me? It literally adds thirty-five years to your life in terms of what you can do. I sometimes get bored now. I don't always know what I'm going to do with myself, but that's a very nice problem to have.

The beauty of real estate is that all the hours of labor are up front. You research and buy a property, and then you rehabilitate it. Then you just need to lease it out and hire a property management company to take care of the rest. After it's set up, you've got an asset that takes you basically zero work hours to generate a passive income. That frees you up to do what you really want to be doing.

Ask yourself if you are fulfilled in your life. Ask yourself if working in corporate America has paid off for you or if you really believe it's going to pay off in the future. Do you think that your job is going to make you rich? Even if you have a fat paycheck, are you rich in terms of savings and assets? Are you rich in terms of time?

I've never really met anybody who became rich in corporate America. I've never met a successful person who works in corporate America. Lots of people think they're successful, but they're really just doing the same thing as everybody else. Maybe you call that success. I call it mediocrity or a modern-day slave.

Do you want to talk about risk? Ninety-nine percent of all people are content to work in corporate America, but corporate work isn't easy. Think how hard it is to climb the corporate ladder. The people you're up against for the big promotion are not idiots. They went to the best colleges. They're smart. Maybe not as smart as you are, but in corporate America you're going to have to work that much harder just to stand out.

But only 1% of people start their own businesses or invest in real estate. If you're only going up against this 1%, right off the bat it's going to be much easier. Add to that the incredible tax savings when you compare real estate with earning a corporate wage. It's a gold mine. The real risk is toiling away in your corporate job with nothing to show for it after forty years.

Think of how many golfers were as good as Tiger Woods in his heyday. Not many you think. He was the best in the world, but how many people had the potential to be as great but just never picked up a club and tried? Just didn't have the opportunity or never sought the opportunity. The point is that you'll never know how great you could've been if you're not willing to try.

I had a passion to try and found business partners who shared my passion. I know many people want more than their corporate job can offer but just can't get over that hump. Not everybody wants that. A lot of people are happy to have a paycheck and go home. They think they're lucky to have a job.

But you shouldn't live your life counting on luck. You shouldn't work hard creating value for your employer and hope he passes some of it back down to you. If you want to break free and start adding value to your own life, then this is the book for you.

I want to help people like you. If you feel that you've been spinning your wheels in a corporate job and don't know how to get out, this is the book for you. If you want to learn how to make more money in real estate than you would have thought possible, this is the book for you. Most importantly, though, if you want to take control of your life and prioritize what truly matters to you, this is the book for you.

This book is a road map for you to take back control of your life. I'm going to tell you what I did to achieve personal freedom and happiness as I could never have imagined possible if I'd stuck with my corporate job. If you can see how the American Dream has become the American Hoax, you're already starting to see the truths that will let you do the same.

Part 1

Starting the Journey

Chapter 1

No Progression

I had a corporate job that seemed the greatest. It was high paying, had the best benefits, and a tidy retirement package waiting for me on the other side. It seemed amazing. Like everything I could have hoped for.

I was really good at my job too. I did better than most people in my position and was paid a little more than most people my age—perhaps $2,000 more a year, and I thought that was very good.

In reality, however, I was simply an idiot. I didn't have the right mind-set. I couldn't see that there was no difference between making $100,000 a year and $102,000, but I bought into the corporate mind-set of the American Dream because that's what I'd been raised to believe. I thought I had it made when I was actually going nowhere.

I was a project manager at a major construction and engineering firm. I majored in construction management, and I got that job right out of college. By the time I quit, I was making roughly $100,000 a year. Many of my friends with similar education and prospects were making $60K or $70K, so I was making a pretty decent amount of money for my age. Everything was on par.

I was also decently high up in the system and was a top-performing project manager for this company. I was in the system. I had a future, but I started to feel something. I started to feel that it wasn't all adding up. I looked to the future that was laid out for me and realized that it wasn't what I wanted.

I knew how much money I was going to make the next year. I knew how much my raises would be. With most corporate jobs, you get an inflationary raise unless you get a different job. Then it might be another $10K. I already knew exactly what my maximum pay was going to be in my life. It was going to be capped somewhere between $200,000 and $300,000. Adjusted for inflation, maybe twenty years down the road it'd be $500,000.

So I knew how much I would make, and I knew where my path was. How exciting, I thought. Here's my whole life laid out before me. Just keep plugging away.

That's not exciting. That's no way to live. I was the definition of a modern day slave. All I had to do was show up ten hours a day, six days a week, for the next 40 years, and my so-called success was all planned out. It was as if I was retired and buried already.

All those incremental raises all laid out in front of me. It was supposed to look like progress, but what was it, really? At thirty, you buy a bigger house. At forty, a better car. It started to look like no progression at all, and it was kind of sad, but it was hard to change my mind-set. It was hard to think of a better way to make money.

Being good at your job makes it that much harder to quit. I was good at my job. I would say I was an exceptional employee. I was making enough money that it was hard to even think about walking away from it. Sometimes I think that people who make less money in their corporate jobs are better off. Having $70K and $200K is really the same in the end, but it's easier to walk away when you only have $70K at stake.

It makes me cringe to see people putting so much effort into getting that next raise or going after their boss's job. The moment you concentrate all your time and energy on getting that next job instead of doing something more productive, you're actually just ruining yourself. It's suicide to strive for another raise. It's nothing. All you'll get is a slightly nicer house, a slightly better car, and you'll just be more stuck. You'll feel more stuck because you're higher in the system, and it'll be harder to walk away.

That's how the reality kicked in. I was three years into my job, and I felt that I was going nowhere. I was fed up and bored and started thinking about ways to extricate myself.

I started doing a lot of research into real estate. I didn't know why at first, but I've always been an entrepreneur at heart. As a child, I was always trying to sell things, and as an adult, I always wanted to figure out how to invest my money. I was buying stocks in college, looking for the next big opportunity, but I only lost money doing that.

I was a few years into my corporate job and thinking about real estate when I decided to take the plunge. My partner and I decided to buy our first rental property. We didn't have any particular experience. I never had a mentor and hadn't taken a course, but I did a lot of reading and research. I didn't go into it ignorant. I taught myself with books and what I read on the Internet.

I paid $60,000 for a college education that was never going to make me any real money. You'd be better off spending a thousand dollars on a real estate seminar or a business seminar if you want to make a lot of money. Who would have thought? Everyone spent so much time making fun of all those gurus out there, and they were the ones who were actually right. They had it all figured out, and everyone else was too blind to notice.

I kept my job, and my partner and I kept investing in real estate. We bought roughly one $100,000 house each year over the next three years, and it was slow going. It's really hard to buy real estate because it's so expensive. It wasn't sexy. It was hard work, but we were building a portfolio, and soon I had this whole stream of revenue coming in apart from my corporate salary.

I decided to go all in before I decided to quit my job. I decided to go off on my own and buy five other rental properties—this time without my partner. This was perhaps six months or a year before I quit my job, and I had ten rental properties altogether. These ten properties produced only $40,000 a year in profit for me, though, so it seemed on paper that it would be a big hit to make them my sole income.

But then my mind-set started to change. I looked at all the problems I had to deal with at my job. I was a construction manager, and each project I was doing was always a hassle. There were always issues dealing with contractors. Nothing was ever easy. It didn't matter what the project involved. I was looking at spending the next thirty-five years of my life doing the same thing, fighting the same fights, having the same arguments. It was going to be the same thing over and over again until I could afford to quit.

But what if I could afford to quit right now? I was only making $40K off my portfolio, but it was tax free, so I was actually making perhaps $80K. I saw how I could grow that. I could see how other people do it—how the 1% thought about making money.

At that time, I was still thinking I could plug away at my corporate job and do real estate on the side. I thought I could do both and be really successful. I could stay in the job I had and make more money than my immediate manager. In just a few years, maybe I would be making as much as a senior executive. I'm just a little guy on the totem pole, but I'm better than they are because I have real estate. I might have carried on like that, but then something happened that pushed me out the door.

They said there was a technical error in my work. It wasn't a scandal or anything especially important, but they were wrong. No one was interested in hearing my side, though, and although they weren't going to fire me, they decided to deduct my bonus at that year's end. So I made $10,000 less than I had the year before.

I was managing a construction site. Our superintendent had to fill out certain safety forms in conjunction with the contractor. My superintendent was actually doing the right thing, but it didn't matter. The word had come down from the top that they had to find places to cut expenses, and my bonus was what someone decided to cut.

This is pretty common in corporate America. Upper management will try to find something to criticize their employees for to keep the herd in line. That year they were deducting bonuses across the board, and I wasn't the only one who lost his bonus. Many people were in the same boat. It wasn't about the actual issue. I was doing the right thing, but they nailed me on whatever pretext they could. It was all about herding cats.

This company was big on bonuses. It was a major part of their compensation package. I was happy to keep working for them. I did good work, and I still had my real estate business on the side, but the bonus issue really irritated me.

It shows how you don't mean anything to them. In the corporate world, you're a cog in the machine. If you think your company cares about you, you're wrong. You're a free asset to them, and they do not really care about you. I hire people, and anyone is replaceable. You ask for a raise and they're looking around for someone who can do everything you can do, only cheaper. I put in thousands of hours of exceptional work for that company, and how did they treat me? They threw me under the bus for something that wasn't even my fault and expected me to accept it.

It doesn't matter how high up in management you are or how many years you've put in with the company. No one is immune to this kind of setup. Even if you're making them money, your boss has no incentive to give you a raise. You're just a line item on a budget, and his bonus depends on shrinking that budget. Losing money, or the threat of it, it's just about keeping you in line.

Losing that bonus really infuriated me, and I realized I had leverage. I had $40,000 coming in from real estate. I wasn't totally dependent on my corporate salary to survive, and even if it was a hit, I was confident I could grow that side of my income.

So I told them to give me my ten grand or I'm leaving. I was ready to quit whether they gave it to me or not, but I didn't tell them that. They probably thought I was making an idle threat because they thought they had all the power in the world over me. They didn't know that I had leverage because of my real estate portfolio.

This experience drove home the reality of power in the corporate system. Robert Kiyosaki calls it modern-day slavery. It's the mind-set of dependence on your salary and corporate job as the only way to get ahead in this world. Your corporate job may not literally enslave you. You're not the property of your bosses, but we're brainwashed to think that there is no other alternative. Corporations earn huge profits off your work, while you have to fight for scraps.

The whole bonus fiasco showed me that I was simply worthless in the broad scheme of the corporate slavery system. They could take away $10,000 of my money for no reason and expect me to come back the next year and try again. If I did something so bad, if I cost them so much, then why not fire me? That's not how they do it. They have various ways to cut your pay and deny you your due to keep you coming back for more, but I was sick of it.

I told them my piece, and an hour later they told me no, and you can leave right now. I was terrified. I didn't know what had just happened. I went home and cried. I thought I had made the biggest mistake of my life.

But that was just the corporate mind-set talking. I was starting to wake up my rational mind, but emotionally it was still incredibly stressful. I was beginning to change mind-sets, but that was a long process still to come. What helped me get over that hump was knowing that I was nothing to the company. I had made that company a lot of money, but they didn't care. They thought that because I didn't fill out a form correctly they could deduct $10K from my bonus. So I was nothing to them.

The entire process of quitting was the hardest thing I've ever done in my life, and I've gotten divorced. It was the most powerful feeling of fear I've ever experienced. I knew I was going against the grain of society. I had been trained my entire life to get the job, do the work, say, "Yes, sir," to the boss, and there I was just quitting on a dime.

The fantasy of quitting is that it will be empowering, which it is, eventually. At first, though, the only thing that is empowered is your fear. The fear of the unknown. The fear of what am I even doing? What is everybody going to think? The fear of what you're giving up.

I questioned myself every day. I would go home and cry. I almost cried at work in front of everybody when I was quitting. I don't even cry, normally, but that's how intense the emotion was. It was unbelievably intense, unlike anything in normal life.

I kept telling myself, though, that I knew what I was doing. I had my rental properties. I had my 401(k) as a safety net. I had my skills and my smarts, and I had books to turn to that helped me see the bigger picture. Tim Ferriss says you need to think of the worst-case scenario. Maybe you go into debt. Maybe you don't pay off your credit cards for a while. I was lucky to have my 401(k), but the most important thing was that I had a plan to grow my assets through real estate.

About a week after I quit in all that turmoil and emotion, it all went away. Partly it was because I knew I could always go back. Get another job if I had to, but I had vowed that I never would. I had worked for one of the best engineering consulting firms in the United States, and I could have gotten another job if I really had to, but I didn't want that anymore.

I was breaking free from corporate America. I was taking control of my life, and for the first time in a long time I felt that I was really progressing toward the kind of life I wanted to lead.

If you work in corporate America, you need to ask yourself what you really want out of life. Most people are too busy working to even think about these things, and once you're in deep, your whole mind-set becomes the job. Your job lingers with you for more than just your eight hours a day. You think about it at night. You think about it on the weekend. Before you know it, it consumes your life. You put all your energy into working on somebody else's creation, and you let your whole life get planned out according to what other people want.

You have to ask yourself if you want more. You have to ask yourself if you want to do the same thing every day for the rest of your life just to get by. If putting all of yourself into a job just to get a slightly nicer house or a slightly better car is worth it to you. If your time and life is worth it.

But if you're waking up and understanding that the American Dream is an American Hoax, then I'm here to tell you that there is a way out.

Chapter 2

The Power of Real Estate

Real estate is all around us, but most people don't really think about it. Most people don't think about it beyond needing a place to live. Maybe you rent somewhere while you're saving up. Then you buy a house. You fix it up. You maintain it. Maybe somewhere down the line you sell it at a profit and use most of that money to buy a bigger, better house. This is the essence of using real estate as a personal savings vehicle, and it's what most people think investing in real estate is all about.

But that's not what I'm talking about.

You also see all these people flipping houses these days. That's where you buy a house, fix it up, and then sell it again the same year. There's a whole cottage industry of television shows and books about flipping.

But that's not what I'm talking about either.

Flipping a house is a full-time job. To make any money at it, you have to put in the hours, and you most likely have to be able do a full renovation by yourself or else you'll be spending all your profits on contractors. On top of that, you'll have to pay 40% on taxes when you sell the property. If you buy the right house in the right neighborhood at the right time and do all the work yourself, maybe you make money flipping houses, but anyone who tells you it's easy or a sure thing is selling you a con.

The way to actually make money on real estate is through rentals. Rental real estate has many advantages over other kinds of real estate investment and over holding a salaried job in the corporate world.

The main advantage involves taxes. The tax advantages of owning rental real estate are astounding. The moment you start buying houses and renting them out you start inventing money. You start inventing cash flow, and that's key to the whole mind-set of making it outside the corporate world.

Rental real estate is also advantageous in terms of leverage. It is the ultimate leveraged investment. The money you borrow to invest in rental real estate will get paid back and turn into profits faster and more easily than business investment. You get similar returns as you would starting a business, but a business only starts being profitable once you build out a complete team that can handle all the work.

Renting properties is straightforward and a practical guarantee on your investment. It is the best way to quickly generate passive income, and it's perfect for anybody who wants to come over to the other side. It's what allowed me to retire at age thirty.

You don't have to have a high net worth. My sweet spot was between $80,000 and $100,000 for a house, which earned me roughly $400 to $500 a month in net profit after all expenses and the mortgage were paid. That may not seem like much, but it's tax free because of the depreciation.

The main things are the tax-free nature of the income and the passive nature of real estate. I bought properties each year while I was still working and built up a solid little portfolio before going all in to make the real money.

These are the things that make rental real estate ideal for the New Rich concept. First articulated by Tim Ferriss, the New Rich is a mind-set for thinking about making money that gets away from the top-down, salaried mind-set that predominates in corporate America.

The key concept of the New Rich mind-set is cash flow. Instead of thinking about money in terms of the fixed salary of the deferred life plan, you have to think about the money flowing in and the money flowing out. To live a life of true freedom, you need to design your cash flow so that you have money coming in through passive income. You build something that will make money without monopolizing your time and attention. That frees you up to focus on what is truly important to you, and it is only at this moment that you can self-actualize what you were put on this earth to do. It is also only at this moment that one person can change the world.

Renting out real estate is an amazing source of passive income. Rent is paid to you monthly. Once you have the property and it's fixed up, the time you have to put into it is minimal. If you hire a professional management company, and you should, the monthly time you need to put into it is basically zero. You just review the financial statement you get from the property manager to make sure nothing's gone wrong. In most cases, that's no more than a five-minute workweek.

Of course, the more property you invest in, the more that everything scales up. If you put a million-dollar apartment building into service, everything's scaled up, and it takes time to get to that point. I invest in apartment buildings now, but I started by renting out a single house with my partner.

But that shows why the power of real estate is so great. What I love most about it is that you feel the effect on your income and on your personal taxes from that first rental property and then from each subsequent property you add to your portfolio. After each property I bought, I was paying less in taxes to the government, which had a domino effect with each house I bought.

The year I quit my job I paid $8,000 through my paycheck to the government in taxes, and I had all $8,000 refunded due to my real estate portfolio. I was able to offset my taxes to corporate America due to my real estate holdings. So real estate is not only tax-free cash flow, but if done correctly with your accountant, it can also offset any other income you have from corporate America. In essence, it increases your corporate salary. It's more than just tax-free income. It makes any other sources of income more tax efficient.

Not only did I make $40,000 tax free from rentals that year, but I also got back my $8,000 in taxes due to the depreciation write-off, and that's not a loophole. It's the same way all over the world. At that point, I was slowly saving on taxes with each new property I bought. The power of all this started to take hold of me. I wanted to scale it up and up to see what would happen if I took it to unknowable proportions.

This is why rental real estate is the most perfect way to earn passive income, which, in turn, allows you to live the New Rich lifestyle. You can do it part-time while still working a corporate job. You can quickly become more successful than your bosses. You can pay less in taxes than your bosses do, and each dollar you make from corporate America becomes more powerful and efficient.

What's important to understand is that the money you earn from rentals is twice as good as the money you earn from your salary because of the tax advantages. Look at it this way. If a real estate investor goes out and buys a $10 lunch, he only pays $10. For someone who only makes money through a corporate salary, that lunch costs them $20. Because to make $10 to pay for lunch, you have to earn $20 on your salary and then give half of that away in taxes and 401(k). For me, a $10 lunch costs $10 because I keep all of what I make.

Rental real estate is also a great way to get started in business. Owning and managing even a single rental property is a great introduction to running a business because it is its own business. A rental property has income, expenses, management. You have to hire vendors. It's a great way to learn how to run your own business, and it will give you a passive income that you can leverage into other opportunities.

But a lot of people look at real estate and wonder if it's risky. I would say that not doing anything and living your life in corporate America is riskier than investing in real estate.

Of course, there are risks, but anything you want do in life has risks. You don't want to buy a bad property. That's why you need to put in the work up front. You need to do your research, and you need to know how to tell the difference between something that will make you money and something that will be nothing but a headache. You might look at a thousand properties before you find the right one. You'll have to go and check out a smaller number of them before you decide on anything, and you need to have good instincts and not just buy into whatever the other person is selling.

The way to manage these risks is to buy right. You might think you don't know how to do that. That's okay. It's something you can learn if you put the time into research. If every week you look at ten properties online and visit one in person and do that for six months, you'll get a sense of what makes a good investment. But you have to take baby steps before you take the plunge if you want to manage the risks.

I have some tips and tricks about how to invest in real estate, but that's not the focus of this book. Many other resources are available that you need to read and research to be successful, for example, there's information about property values and demographics and neighborhood trends that you need to investigate. I'll tell you a few of my secrets in this book, but this should be the first thing you read before doing all the work that comes after. The point of this book is to show you the lifestyle you can have, the mind-set that you'll need, and the strategies that will help you succeed after you quit your job.

I recommend that you start slowly. Keep your job for a while and start with houses. Start with a single house. My partner and I spent an entire year saving up $10,000 for a down payment. We only added one house per year for three years after that. It was hard work. It was very slow and unsexy, but once we'd reached a critical mass, things started to speed up.

Once I put in the work and got something going, there was no stopping me.

Looking back, there are ways I would have done things differently to speed things up, but that's the value of experience. I can tell you how I did it, and it worked, but I can also tell you how to do it better than I did.

With every acquisition, you're going to become more powerful. You'll soon be better off economically than anyone else in corporate America, including your bosses and your bosses' bosses. You can walk around with a smile on your face, knowing you're better off than your boss. How empowering is that. You'll feel it in your wallet.

The biggest advantage of rental real estate is the time it provides. All the time is up front in terms of researching, but even that isn't so much. It is easily possible to do that while still putting in forty hours a week at a corporate job. But as soon as you've built up enough of a portfolio that you don't need the corporate job anymore, the whole world opens up to you. You'll have so much free time that you won't know what to do with yourself. You'll start companies. You'll travel. You'll do all the things you've ever wanted to do. It's going to be addictive.

Real estate is the quickest way to become financially free in the world today, and you don't have to be rich to get into real estate. You could have a net worth of $0 and still have enough cash flow to be financially free. Financial freedom doesn't come from being rich. It comes from having a positive cash flow, and the quickest way to get that kind of cash flow is through real estate.

It's much harder to start an online company or any company for that matter while still working a full-time job, but it is entirely possible to generate passive income from real estate with only a minimal investment of time.

That's the power of real estate. Real estate is your access. It's your portal to the 1%, and, most importantly, it's the way you get from the employment paycheck mind-set to the New Rich mind-set. To the cash flow mind-set.

I remember my first rental property. My partner and I worked with a local real estate agent to find a property. We'd been looking at so many places on the Internet. We'd gone out to see a few of them in person, and we found one place that was a foreclosure. It was a townhouse, so it was combined with other units. It had three bedrooms, one and a half baths, but it was a mess and needed a lot of work. That was part of what scared us. We didn't know what we were doing. Up until that point, we were just looking at properties.

It was so cheap because it was so bad. It was listed at around $45,000, but we knew we could rent it for $1,100 a month if we fixed it up. So we offered $38,000, but it was extremely nerve-wracking.

We didn't have any experience. Both of us were married and had our own houses, but we didn't know how to do anything except a little bit of housework. We did know, however, that we could fix it up on our own if we put the time and money into it. We believed it could be profitable.

After we had it inspected, we learned that it was really bad. There was termite damage and all these other things that we hadn't seen ourselves. It looked bad to our eyes, but to hear it was even worse and dispiriting. We didn't know if we should go for it, so I called my partner on the phone, and we had a conversation that changed my life.

We had to sign a contract to own this property, and then we would still need to put $10,000 worth of work into it before we could rent it out. It was extremely stressful, but I still had my corporate job to fall back on at that point.

I'll never forget our conversation. We were almost going to back out. The inspection had come back, and we learned about all these issues that we hadn't expected. Looking back now, they weren't even that important, but I didn't know any better at the time. My partner and I had no idea what we were doing. We were outside of our comfort zone, and my partner was talking us out of the deal.

But I said, "Stop. If we don't buy this property, we will never do this again. I don't give a fuck about anything else."

That's the mind-set you have to have. I don't care if I lose this $10,000. I don't care if I look ridiculous, and I don't care about what anyone else will say. At least you're doing something. At least you tried.

And we did try. And we made it.

Not blindly or because we were lucky, but we did the work. We did the research. We took our chance, and we made it.

That was a freaky property. You can't really find anything that cheap anymore, but that one conversation got us into the deal, and once we started, all those things that had seemed disqualifying turned out to be not that important after all. The termite damage? That cost $300 to deal with. We repainted and redid some flooring. Everything turned out to be cheaper than we expected. It turned out that this property that we thought was the end of the world was like the textbook definition of a rental property. We spent about $42,000 all in and had it rented out within two months for $1,100. We wound up selling it in two years for $60,000 because a better opportunity came up.

It's a success story of overcoming fear and realizing the potential of something. Unless you're an avid quitter, you can accomplish what you set out to do. All you need is a little intelligence and a bit of hard work. It's especially motivating when it's your own money on the line.

That's why I highly recommend that you just dive in. What else are you going to do with 10 grand? Invest in the stock market and make a tiny return if you're lucky? It's much better to go after something that will change your life. That one property, that one conversation. We figured it out. We learned so much that made it that much easier for our next property. All you have to do is make a decision.

That decision is what made me who I am today. If it'd gone the other way, I'd still be working for that company. I never would've quit. Nothing would have happened.

There are moments that define your whole life. That was one of them. That was when I decided to go all in. That was when I decided I wouldn't be the same as everybody else.

Fast-forward three years and that property was extremely profitable. We bought it for $38,000. We ended up selling it for $60,000, and it provided us with two years of $500/month or $6,000/year tax-free cash flow. Talk about getting addicted. After that, I wanted to buy more. I wanted to build something. I wanted to break free.

You've got to stay true to your guns and your guts. If you don't, you'll back out. You'll just stay like everybody else. That conversation was what changed my life. Just a phone call between potential partners. We were like two scared little puppies, but we did it, and the rest is history. We started something, and it took me places I could never have imagined.

Chapter 3

Building a Portfolio and Taking the Plunge

The way to get started in real estate is by educating yourself. Reading this book is a good start. It will help you make the change in mind-sets that is essential to succeeding in the New Rich lifestyle, but while this is the first book you should read, it is not the only one. This is just to get started.

When you finish this book, go out and buy another book on real estate. Read it, and then go out and buy another. Many such books are available. Some will provide useful information, while others will just sell a story. The only way to tell a good book from a bad one is to read everything. Make yourself an expert on the subject. Then you'll be able to recognize the good from the bad.

You should also do other things. You can do research on the Internet. You can take a course from a guru. Again, good and bad sources of information are available, but only by educating yourself can you develop the tools to let you tell the difference.

I got started through aggressive Internet research, day and night. I spent time on a message board to connect with like-minded people and get a sense of where I could find good information. The message board I used was called BiggerPockets.com, which connected people new to real estate investment with experts. It transformed my life. I never had a role model, no one walking me through it. I just learned on the Internet and taught myself through reading and research.

Books and websites can be your mentor if you pick the right ones. You don't need someone walking you through every little step, and you don't need to pay someone a lot of money to tell you what to do. Books can be your mentors. You can find mentors in online communities. It can be many different things. It doesn't have to be an actual person.

You also don't need a lot of money to invest in real estate. If you want to do it conservatively and minimize your risks, you need about $10,000 for your first down payment, but you can do it with less.

You can work with a partner as I did to split up that initial investment. Our first property needed about a $20,000 investment, so we each put in $10K, but it was certainly easier than putting in $20,000 by myself. If you don't have that much money, you can start with a cheaper property. Again, what's important is to get that cash flow moving. So long as the money is coming in, you can save up to invest in the next property and the one after that.

Some people say you can get into real estate with $0 out of pocket. That might work out for some people, but it is very uncommon. It's better to save up a bit of money to cover that initial down payment. If you don't have the money, you're better off leveraging credit card debt, using a home equity line of credit, or getting a loan from family and friends. I have used all three.

I financed my first deal partly through a credit card, but you need to tread lightly. During the acquisition phase of my first investment, I had to pull $5,000 off a credit card because I was short on cash. Theoretically, you could put the whole

$20,000 down payment on a credit card and be able to buy property with $0 down, but that is not recommended. People aren't good with credit cards, which is a shame because they are an amazing tool for managing your finances, but you can't treat them like free money. It's better to use savings for your initial investment. If you know what you're doing, though, you can run a little credit card debt as I did.

Tim Ferriss says that the worst-case scenario of investing in your dreams is going into credit card debt. When you put it that way, it's not so bad. You can walk away from credit card debt. Not that I ever have, but it's possible. The point is that you can neither be too reckless nor too conservative when it comes to credit cards. They are a tool that you can use to get started in real estate, but you have to be smart about it.

Partnerships are also a great way to get started. Sometimes you can find a partner who has the cash but doesn't have the time or interest in doing the setup work. Tell them you'll do all that work. You'll rehab it, lease it out, and manage it if they provide the down payment. That's another way to get started without any money.

A good rule of thumb with a partner, though, is to split everything 50/50. If you and your partner work in corporate America, saving up ten grand in a year is more than possible. It may seem like a lot. It did for me. It was my entire savings for a year, but you just have to remember that the dollars you put toward that down payment will come back to you every month for as long as you own the property. Every night you stay in to save money during that year is paying for your financial liberation.

You have to remember, however, that building a portfolio is hard. Even if you manage to keep saving $10,000 and buying a new property every year, it will still seem like a long way off until you can retire on that income. That's why it's important to find ways to add value to your investment if you really want to accelerate growth.

Adding value is the key idea behind the flipping approach to real estate. You've seen this on TV. Buy the house, do the renovation, resell it for big profits. But flipping is not the best thing you could be doing from a tax perspective. That's why I say you have to flip a house theoretically but then actually rent it out.

What happens when you do this? You increase the value, you increase your equity in the investment, and you increase your cash flow.

When I buy a house, I put the time and money into rehabilitating it because it was probably a foreclosure or it was in poor condition and not living up to its true potential. Then I rent it out again. All the money you put in starts coming back to you. Pretty soon, you're making a profit off your investment.

How do you speed this up? How do you expand your portfolio to the point that you can live off it? More importantly, how do you keep investing in real estate when it's so capital intensive?

Well, there's a secret to that, but it's something that all professional real estate investors know—all real estate is actually free. ALL REAL ESTATE IS FREE, and I'm going to tell you why that's so.

By the time we hit our three-year mark, we had three houses that we'd acquired and rehabilitated. We didn't see immediate profits from flipping because we were renting them out, building a steady cash flow. At the three-year mark, we refinanced all three properties. We got back all our down payments and repair money plus $50K, so the total cash at closing was $110K tax free to us.

Then we took that money and purchased three more houses, doubling the size of our portfolio. This simultaneously doubled our monthly cash flow in one fell swoop! The goal is to acquire, rehab, rent, and refinance as quickly as possible to immediately grow your portfolio.

You have to refinance real estate at all costs. When people tell you that the debt is bad debt, they're wrong. It's not bad debt. It'll make you richer than your wildest dreams—so long as you keep buying more properties and reinvesting all monies.

At first, it seemed that it'd be impossible to scale, but over time, the properties increased in value, and our mortgages were paid down. We could put more money into rehab and charge higher rents. We paid down the mortgage bit by bit. By the three-year point, we were in a position to double the size of our portfolio.

Adding value is the way you scale real estate. You've got to add value through rehabilitation. You've got to refinance to get back your original capital to reinvest. Before acquiring any real estate, your first questions should be when do I get my money back and when can I refinance my entire investment out of this deal while keeping the asset.

Once I understood how it worked, I was ready to go off on my own. I saw how I could quit my job and make it work. I didn't have the cash flow in place yet, but I could see how to get there.

That's how real estate investors with minimal capital can become multimillionaires. It's because they buy the real estate. After one month for houses and one to three years for apartment buildings, they refinance every single dime ever invested in that project out of the deal while maintaining the asset and the cash flow it represents. So your money is not locked away forever. By adding value to your real estate, you can use refinancing to have a FREE asset that produces cash flow, mortgage buydown, and tax savings for the rest of your life.

This was the OMG moment of my real estate career. This was the question I asked myself once I figured this out:

"If all real estate is free, how much can you acquire?"

The answer:

"As much as I can get my fucking hands on!!!"

Currently, I own more than three hundred units across eight apartment buildings. I have refinanced my entire investment out of all eight of them. This portfolio produces more than $300K annually in tax-free cash flow, and I have none of my own money in any of these deals.

29

It's also worth noting that each apartment building is on non-recourse debt. This means that even if I defaulted on the loan, the bank cannot come after me or foreclose on me personally.

So what just happened? I have none of my capital at risk in any of these deals, and I am not liable for any of the mortgages even if I defaulted. All while myself and my partners receive $300K+ tax-free income, monthly mortgage buy-down, and massive annual tax savings on a $12 million portfolio.

I know, right? Talk about zero risk, right??? This is where you want to be.

I have these assets that will continue to generate cash flow and make me a passive income. Refinancing is essential to freeing up the capital to invest in more properties. That's the secret to building a portfolio. Refinancing allows you to pull your money out while maintaining the asset, cash flow, tax savings, and principle buydown.

This is something that everybody can do. I bought my first five properties while maintaining a full-time job. I was managing those properties myself, and even still it didn't take that much time. As you get a bigger portfolio, you'll need to transfer to third-party management, but by that point you don't really have to do anything. Just sit at home and wait for the money to show up in your mailbox.

I recommend that you start small. My sweet spot is a $50K to $100K house that rents for $1,000 to $1,500 a month. Regardless of the price point, however, be sure you put the money into rehabilitation. Adding value gets you money back faster, meaning that you can invest in more properties and grow your portfolio. Then you'll be able to keep growing for the rest of your life.

Don't be discouraged if you face challenges along the way because you will. I made many mistakes that I shouldn't have.

The biggest mistake was buying a $20,000 house in the middle of the ghetto. It looked good on paper. Many properties in bad areas appear to be cash kings, but they won't be. The time expense is so bad. You'll lose money, and it'll be a headache even if you hire third-party management. I probably lost $10,000 on that deal. You've got to stay away from such properties.

Find something in a good school district. Somewhere between $50,000 and $100,000 is what you should look for, and you want white-collar tenants. People with families renting from you. The kind of people you worked with in corporate America. People living the American Dream.

You must also be careful when you hire a property manager. You can handle up to five properties yourself, which you should do so that you know what to expect from a third party.

Houses are unique because they reduce your risk, and you always have the option to resell them to a family or an investor. Now, I invest in apartment buildings for economies of scale and the non-recourse debt that comes with a $1 million+ loan. The only people I sell those to are other investors. Houses are easier for getting started. Not only do they reduce your risk with several exit plans, but they also retain their value really well. This gives you two outs. You can sell to an investor, or you can sell to a normal family. There's always a market for a house in a good neighborhood that you've rehabilitated.

When I started doing this full-time, though, I knew I wanted to get into apartment buildings. That was hard. It was an entirely different ball game from houses. I was out of my comfort zone, but I needed to move up to the next level.

I actually ended up buying my first apartment building. It cost a million dollars, but I found out that it was easier to get a one-million-dollar loan for this type of property than it was to get a $100,000 loan for a house. I couldn't believe it, but it's easier to get money as an investor than as a homeowner. I used part of my 401(k), and I was set.

I also listed all ten of the houses I had at that point. I put them all up for sale as a portfolio of rental properties. I sold them all and then rolled them into apartment buildings, buying two more on top of the one I previously purchased. All of it tax free. That's the beauty of real estate. That's the power of the 1031 exchange.

You can sell in and out of real estate tax free through a 1031 exchange. You're constantly refinancing the money out of the deal and selling when you want to. It allows you to roll the profit and depreciation into bigger buildings, which will amplify your portfolio and your cash flow. It's a constant cycle of growth. Pay no tax, buy bigger, and your cash flow goes up. As you can imagine, you can build up quite the portfolio over a lifetime. This is how billionaires are born.

Many people think that location, location, location is the only thing you need to know about real estate. A good location is nice, but that's not where you'll get the best return. The real mantra should be: ADD VALUE, ADD VALUE, ADD VALUE. The moment you're adding value is the moment you can bring your money out quicker and double your income. Every time you refinance your income will double. If you add value, you can do it as quickly as a month.

After I had figured it out, it was easy for me to buy a house in cash, fix it up with cash, and refinance it in one month. That was because I knew houses so well. Before I even leased it, I had all my money back. It was like buying houses for nothing. That's the expert level.

The best house investment I ever made was all about this. I added so much value to this house that I walked away with a check for $10K at closing. The house wasn't free. It was actually more than free. They paid me $10K to take over a cash flow asset, and this happens all the time. I have seen my investor friends rehab apartment buildings so well that they walk away with hundreds of thousands of dollars after refinancing, all while the apartment building was on non-recourse debt, and the cash was flowing nicely!

Apartment buildings are more exciting, but they're the next level. They're economies of scale, but the best advice to get started is to not think about the endgame. The way to eat an elephant is one bite at a time. You need to build your knowledge and make smart decisions. Start with a single house and build from there.

You need to develop a new way of thinking. You have to wait for the right moment and be ready to act when it comes. Do your research. Do the work. Have a plan. Then you can get serious. Then you can buy your first rental property.

There'll be a turn in your thinking. Your mind will open up to a new world of possibilities. You can't act as if you're going to be some big mogul right at the very beginning. You have to take baby steps.

But then you'll be ready to take the plunge and be free.

Part 2

There Will Be Blood

Chapter 4

Quitting and the Aftermath

When I was getting ready to quit my job, I had ten rental properties and making exactly $40,000 a year in cash flow from these assets. Still, the decision to quit was extremely difficult.

It was harder than my divorce. Getting divorced was like quitting your job but staying in corporate America. It was hard, but you knew in the back of your mind that you would get another job. Have another relationship. The way I was quitting was like turning my back on everything I'd been raised to believe. It wasn't just getting a divorce. It was becoming a monk. It wasn't just quitting a job. It was quitting work. Or at least what everybody else thinks of as work. It was not easy.

It was the hardest decision of my life. The only reason I could even think of doing it was because I had this portfolio of ten properties. That was my lifeline, and I didn't think I had any other choice. After that business with the bonus, I knew I couldn't stay there for the rest of my life.

Real estate gave me an opportunity. It gave me lots of opportunities. I had other things going on, so I didn't have to accept the shabby treatment I got from corporate America.

Emotionally, however, it was still hard. When you've been taught your whole life that the world is one way, it can be nearly impossible to go against the grain. The idea of the corporate job—of the American Dream—is so drilled into us that it seems insane to try anything else. Even if you know it's not working for you and that there are alternatives, it's hard to feel that you're doing the right thing.

It was extremely terrifying to quit. I was giving up an amazing job. I knew I wasn't going to get my bonus back, but the money barely even mattered anymore. I wasn't even thinking about that. I felt that I'd been standing on the edge of a cliff, and I'd convinced myself to jump off. Even though rationally I knew that I had a parachute in the form of my real estate portfolio, I felt that I was plunging into oblivion.

I was so scared that I went home and cried. As I've said, I'm not a crier. It's not a normal reaction for me to have, but that's what happened. That's what I felt. That's how much turmoil quitting put me through. It was as if I didn't even know who I was anymore.

A week later, though, there was no fear. I was over it. I knew what I had to do, and I knew how to make it happen. It was time to go to work. I had to start buying real estate and build up my portfolio. That's what I had to put all my time into.

So it was one of the saddest times in my life but also one of the most exciting.

I threw myself into the business. I started to think about it as a business. As something I put so many hours into each day. I had a new project, and I was working toward a goal.

Soon enough, three months had gone by. I was doing well, and I was feeling great about it. Then I was talking with my mother one day and realized that she didn't know what had happened. She still thought I worked for the company. So now I had to tell my family.

That was fun. It was about the last thing they would have expected. I knew they were going to go through all the things I'd gone through, only on an accelerated timeline.

By that point, I'd been doing real estate on the side for several years. I'd spent the three months since I quit setting up new deals. From my perspective, everything was starting to come into focus, but from an outside observer steeped in the dogma of the American Dream, I had some explaining to do.

The important thing was that I was in the right mind-set to tell them. I was happy. I was confident in my success. You don't want to tell your family the day you quit. When you're at peak emotional turmoil. You want to be past the sadness and have everything together when you tell people something like this.

My folks were shocked to say the least. My mother—God bless her heart—couldn't believe it. She was upset. She was angry. She asked me why they had even paid for my college. I give her a lot of credit. She's one of the best people in the world, and she thought I was set up for life, but she was literally mad at me.

My dad's reaction was another story. In essence, "Best of luck, man." And that was it. My dad's my biggest fan, but my mother was a tough cookie, but she came around, too, after I explained it all and showed them what I'd been doing.

Maybe I shouldn't have told them at Christmas that I'd been out of work for three months. They were going about their lives, thinking everything was still the same with me. It was a very interesting, emotionally honest situation we found ourselves in. But you should definitely wait for the opportune moment to tell your family and especially your extended family.

With your spouse, obviously, it's different. She should know immediately when you make such a fundamental economic decision. She's someone you should be talking with about your plans long before you quit. For other family members, however, I would advise that you wait at least a month before telling them so that they can see the best possible version of what you'll be doing.

People aren't going to understand. They won't understand that you've been living a fantasy because odds are that they are still living that fantasy. That's the power of the American Hoax. They'll think that the only way to have a secure future is to plug yourself into that corporate job for forty years.

They'll tell you that playing with real estate is the fantasy. They'll tell you that retiring at age thirty is a fantasy, but they're wrong. Corporate America is the fantasy. Owning property and running your own business is reality.

It's extremely scary to turn the world upside down. It'll seem scary to the people in your life, but those fears go away, and nothing convinces people like success. By the time I told my family what I was up to, I was about to start buying apartment buildings. I already knew what I was doing, and I could show it.

You'll find that after the initial shock everybody has advice for you when it comes to real estate. Some of that will be useful. A lot of it will not. You don't want people coming to you every day with unsolicited advice. That quickly becomes too much to handle, and you'll find yourself putting in a lot of emotional labor that you don't need managing other people's anxieties.

You also need to work on yourself. Emotionally, it's going to be a battle. You need to be healthy. You need to be happy. You need to be your own biggest cheerleader because there's no shortage of people out there who'll say that you won't succeed.

It's extremely difficult. It's a change in mind-set and a change in lifestyle, but if you take care of yourself and put in the work, you'll find that it's more rewarding than corporate work ever was. You'll find for the first time in your life that you're financially free.

Chapter 5

Adjusting to a New Life

After I quit and worked through all that turmoil, I had to adjust to a life where I didn't report to anybody. I was accountable only to myself, and I could do whatever I wanted in the world.

That's the dream, right? Well, it was a very empowering feeling, but it was also kind of scary because then you're the only one in charge. The buck stops with you. Whether you succeed or fail is all up to you. The feeling is incredible. You have so much free time that you don't even know what to do with yourself, but if you don't quickly develop self-discipline, you're going to blow your shot.

The reality is that you become the master of your own domain. If you have bad habits, those are going to be magnified. There's no one to say do this now or don't do that or you'll lose your job. You have to be the one to motivate yourself. You have to adjust yourself to the New Rich lifestyle.

So it becomes essential to keep yourself on target. There's no one to report to. The options to fill your day are limitless, but you have to make sure that every day you're doing what you need to do to keep the cash flow coming in and growing.

The world may seem a little lonely at first. Everyone you know who still works a corporate job will be busy all day while you're sitting at home doing your own thing. There's no structure to your job now. Sometimes you'll want to view a property and the owner will only be available at some odd hour. You have to work when you need to, not according to some regular schedule.

You have to figure out how to be happy with this when you've been grinding your entire life. With real estate, you will have a lot more free time in general that you'll need to fill in ways that make you happy. You'll pick up new hobbies. You'll go places. You'll meet new people who work atypical hours, but it can be tougher to live this way.

That's one thing corporate America has going for it. It keeps you active and social. Your life is scheduled for you, and you develop friendships with the people you work with. You need to replicate the positive social aspects of corporate work as much as possible. Develop a schedule that works for you. See people. Work out, play golf, travel. Try to do more with your time. You'll find it easier because you won't be exhausted from the daily grind all the time.

There's a big learning curve that starts the moment you quit your job. You're financially free. You're the master of your own domain, and it's up to you to determine if your domain is too tough to handle or if you're on top of the world.

It's critical that you stay true to yourself and cultivate your good habits. You have to really concentrate to make sure your bad habits don't take over your life because it's easy to go the wrong way when you have enough free time and there's no one else in charge of your life.

That's actually something I'm still working on even now. I still have to work to find enough things to fill my day that fulfill me. Real estate doesn't take as much time as people think. So you have to devote yourself to becoming a better person. I'm constantly thinking about eating right, working on my body, developing hobbies, golf, sports, travel, you name it—but these are good problems to have.

The biggest challenge is staying social. It is so easy to feel lonely when everyone you know is working a corporate job and you're not. That's something I'm still working on. It drives you a little crazy, and it shows how much the corporate mindset consumes a person's whole life. You'll see people who have nothing to talk about except their jobs. It'll start to seem a little sad when that's all people can even think about.

In the first year, I would find myself sitting on the couch every day around 1:00 in the afternoon with nothing to do. I got up and did my work the first thing in the morning, but I was out of things to do by the afternoon. You find yourself just sitting and watching TV. That's when the doubts creep in. That's when you ask yourself, "Am I a joke? What am I doing with my life?" You feel yourself starting to become lazy, but that's the freedom you've done all this for. That's the result of leveraging your assets to free up your time.

Tim Ferriss said that being too busy is actually a form of laziness. You feel lazy and worthless, when the truth is that you're making all this money out of nothing. People who work all the time and lead these lives of perpetual busy-ness are the lazy ones because they're not getting the most out of life. They are taking what was given to them and accepting it without question. It's only when you free up your time that you really start thinking productively. You're free to think outside the box. You'll start to self-actualize. This is what we were really put on this earth to do.

You'll start companies. I started private label companies that now make more money than my real estate investments. I did that because I had the time and the money to make something new.

You'll go places. You could just travel the world forever without coming back for anything. You can go after anything in life without being constrained.

You'll get so bored that your body will make you do it. Your mind will be active as it never was before, and you'll just be coming up with new ideas that will make you money. Ideas for new businesses or real estate or whatever. Maybe you'll come up with a new way to buy your next investment property. You will be constantly thinking about ways to improve your own wealth.

I can barely even describe the difference in my thinking. I spent years on this while I was still working my corporate job. I was making money, but it was slow. After quitting, that's when the real entrepreneur comes out because he has nothing else to distract him. He has nothing else to do. Nothing else but to make money.

For the first six months after I quit, boredom was a real problem. I wasn't married. I was single at the time, which probably didn't help, but even if you are married or have a girlfriend and she goes to work, you're still by yourself all day.

You second-guess yourself when you're on your own like that. It's natural. Maybe it's inevitable, but that's part of the learning experience. You need to learn how to fill that void.

You need to learn how to stay on target. You need to learn how to be free and thrive, which is harder than people think.

But what does my life look like? I think it looks pretty good.

I take my dog for more walks. I go to coffee shops every morning and socialize with the regulars. I've been on multimonth backpacking trips to Southeast Asia, Europe, and I'm planning one for South America. I constantly work on myself. I work out every day. I play golf. I find new clothes.

This may sound silly, but I always go shopping for new clothes. I'm constantly working to fill the void. I try to figure out which are the best boxers. I want the best shirt. I want the best workout clothes. I want the best haircut.

I want people to see me when I walk around and say that guy's polished. I don't want people to see me and think that I work from home, and it's funny what you start doing when you have a little money to spare. I like to experiment with things. Buy different products and compare them. See which one is best.

I started cooking every meal. I still go out to eat when I want to meet people and socialize, but I wanted to be able to eat right and cook well. I wanted to develop that skill in myself.

It's funny how when you're working that you're too busy to eat out with people. I get this all the time now. Can't meet up, too tired. Just going home to order delivery. How out of whack is that? These jobs work you so hard that you can't even enjoy a meal out with friends not to mention having no time to cook a decent meal. It's no wonder there's an obesity epidemic in this country.

When you quit your job, though, you can fill your day with living. For the first time in your life, you'll be free to do the things you want to do. You'll take care of yourself. You'll improve yourself. Pretty soon it will seem crazy to have lived any other way.

But you have to fill up your day to get the most out of it. You can't let the devil in. The devil gets in when you're by yourself for too long, when you let your thoughts turn back on themselves. If you sit by yourself for too long, you're going to second-guess yourself even if what you're doing is exactly right.

So you've got to get the devil out of there, and you do that by staying active and doing things, especially with other people.

Chapter 6

The Cash Flow vs. Paycheck Mind-sets

Before I quit, I had been a top-notch corporate American worker my entire life. I did everything right. I commanded a good salary, especially for my age. The company I worked at paid healthy bonuses, and I'd been taught to believe that was the only way to live.

I could not imagine life without a paycheck. That's a major impediment to quitting your job. You think that without this paycheck coming in there's no way that you can live, but that is part of the mind-set of corporate America.

You can actually think of real estate income as a monthly paycheck. Instead of every two weeks, you get a deposit every month that grows as you expand your portfolio, but that's only a half measure. You really have more control over your income with real estate than you ever do with a corporate paycheck. To understand that, you need to understand the difference between cash flow and paycheck mind-sets.

Robert Kiyosaki is someone to read if you want to understand the cash flow mind-set. Simply put, the cash flow mind-set is that you have an asset that will provide you with the money you need to live. It's not about people working a certain number of hours or accomplishing a certain number of projects. It's about building businesses or real estate assets that will provide you with a steady cash flow that will support you.

It sounds straightforward, but it's really not. The extent to which we're indoctrinated into the paycheck mind-set is staggering. We're told that anyone without a paycheck is a bum or lazy, but real laziness is plugging into the system without maximizing your potential.

The reality is that changing mind-sets is the hardest part of quitting. You can be the best real estate investor in the world, and you can be making a considerable amount of money, but you'll still think you can't quit your job because you're stuck in the paycheck mind-set.

The cash flow mind-set is thinking about the money flowing in and the money flowing out. It's about calculating how much money you need coming in to fund the life you want. When you think about it in those terms, you'll be surprised how little you actually need to fund a good life.

Say you have a $100,000 a year salary from a corporate job. Sounds like a lot of money, right? But where does it go? You buy the house, you buy the car. Save for your children's tuition. Your retirement. Two weeks' vacation once a year. Suddenly, it doesn't seem like so much. That's why there are people pulling in huge paychecks who are still cash poor. That's why there's someone earning twice as much as you are who's no better off.

The moment you give up the paycheck mind-set and completely dedicate yourself to the cash flow mind-set, you're going to make so much more. You'll do more with less money. If you invest in rental real estate, you'll have amazing tax savings. You'll think about money coming in and spend it on what really matters to you. You'll be so much better off.

What about risk? Isn't the paycheck a sure thing and real estate a gamble? That's the American Dream talking. That's the paycheck mind-set.

What's most risky is depending entirely on a paycheck. That's the abdication of control. If your corporate bosses decide, they can deduct $10K from you as they did to me. That's pretty risky. You could get fired. Maybe not even for any good reason. Maybe just to save the higher ups a few percentage points in their budgets so that they get the big bonuses. Such things happen all the time.

The corporation does not care about you. You are just an asset for them to exploit. You'll be tossed aside the moment it seems that you cost them more than you make them. You are totally at their beck and call. That's the riskiest way to live.

When you own your own business, you're in control. You pay less in taxes. You have the ability to produce more money with less work. You have the opportunity to try new things and diversify. I got started in real estate, and now I'm starting other kinds of companies. You will have the time and the capacity to think about new ways to increase your cash flow.

The cash flow mind-set is saying you don't need a paycheck because your business assets are going to provide you the money you need to live. It's about having a steady stream of income that allows you to focus on the next big thing. You might start a company that's the next big thing and sell it off to take care of you for the rest of your life. The cash flow mind-set is perfect for the Internet Age.

In the Industrial Age, everyone relied on paychecks, but the Internet Age is the age of cash flow. It's never been easier to make a million dollars. You don't even need to have the best idea. You can get any product in front of so many people so easily that it's easy to make money.

I'm lucky enough to have done this. Who knows where I'll be by the time I'm 40? The cash flow mind-set creates unlimited possibilities for people in every field. It puts you in control of your life in a way that isn't possible in the paycheck model. It will set you free.

When you have a corporate job, you do what they tell you when they tell you to do it. If they need someone to go overseas for two months, you do it. If they need someone to work late, you do it. Never mind that your child's baseball game starts at 5:30. It's your job, and they pay you just enough—just enough that you think it's worth it, just enough that you can't ever quit.

The moment you give that up, it'll change your entire life. You're going to see a world of opportunity, but changing mind-sets is harder than you think. You read this and nod along. You've always felt that it didn't quite add up, but that paycheck mind-set is in you so deep. You can sabotage yourself if you let it creep back in. You'll hear it in your loneliest moments, filling your head with doubt.

That's why it's better to transition slowly. Buy some rental properties while you still have your corporate job. See how it works. Put your paycheck money and your rental income money into two separate categories. Cultivate the cash flow mind-set in that part of your life, and slowly wean yourself off that paycheck.

No one can wake up one morning and say, "Oh, I'm going to live off cash flow." That's not how it works. I've never met anybody who could do that. You have to see cash flow in action. Get some rental properties. Start your own company on the side. Get a taste for it. It can be highly addictive. You'll want to dive in all at once, but be patient and do it right, and things will go so much better for you.

In my experience, the best way to change mind-sets is by reading books. The first book I read was *Rich Dad, Poor Dad* by Robert Kiyosaki. I read the entire book in one sitting. I started at 5:00 p.m. and couldn't put it down until 3:00 the next morning. I already had five rental properties at that point. I was groping my way looking for this other way to live, and this book got me thinking about it in a systematic way. It showed me I wasn't crazy. It showed me that other people were doing this, and it gave me the confidence to act deliberately.

That was just the first taste. That was the beginning of my real education—of my mind-set shift. I read forty more books that year. That's what it took for me to see the whole world differently, but you need to be open to it. It's one thing to read a good book, but it's another to read it at the right time in your life. *Rich Dad, Poor Dad* was the right book for me at the right time in my life. I felt that I was already doing what he was preaching. I felt he was speaking my language—that he was just as smart as I was.

This change in mind-sets is vitally important at this moment. The paycheck mind-set may have worked in the Industrial Age, but things are different now. The middle class is struggling. Big business has found it doesn't have to be so generous to keep people working for them. Something is wrong. Young people today don't believe they will get a job for life that will give them a steady paycheck, and they're right. Things aren't going to be as they have been before.

The Internet has been an absolute game changer. We don't even think about it anymore, but every day people have immediate access to information about so many things that they never have before. The Internet was an invaluable resource for me getting into real estate. I can sit on the toilet and research properties, learning so much from just the palm of my hand.

The knowledge is so great, and everybody has an opportunity to access it. You can become an expert in any subject really quickly, but you won't have time to seize these new opportunities if you're burning time at a corporate job.

The cash flow mind-set is the future. Everybody needs to adopt it, or you'll be left behind. Don't expect your corporate bosses to take care of you. Don't expect your paycheck to always be there.

The riskiest thing you can do is carry on like nothing changed because everything has changed.

Part 3

Freedom, Fulfillment, and Financial Independence

Chapter 7

Real Estate as the Ideal Asset Class

Buying a house is part of the American Dream. It's a really big part. The white-picket fence in the suburbs, the place you raise your children. More importantly, buying a house is a savings mechanism in the American Dream. You buy a house to live in. You maintain it and fix it up. Eventually, you'll be able to sell it at profit because its value has increased, and you paid down the mortgage. For many people, selling their house is central to their retirement plan.

I had that all lined up when I was working my corporate job. I was already buying a house before I even had the job. That was the plan. Get the job. Buy the house. Live, work, retire.

Well, let me tell you something. Buying a new house is the biggest hoax in the history of the world.

There is an epidemic of misinformation about this subject. Buying a house is not really an investment. It's a liability. It's just like renting but actually much worse because you have to give up your capital for a down payment, and anybody who tells you that buying a house is the best investment you'll ever make is selling you a story.

I've never seen more destruction of wealth in my life as when people put all their savings as a down payment on a house when they're single or even when you're just married. If you're just starting out, there's no reason to do that. People are only convinced of that because they've bought into the American Dream.

If you put a $60K down payment into a personal residence and don't live in it for more than ten years, you at best break even when compared with renting, and you're not going to live in the house you buy when you're twenty for more than ten years. You're not going to live in the house you buy when you're just married for that long. Your family will grow. You'll need more space, and the opportunity costs of parking all your money in a house you won't keep are astounding.

Your $60K down payment should not go into your personal residence. It should be invested in rental properties or starting a company. Then, in five to ten years, you can buy that starter home in CASH!

Renting gets a bad rap in this country, but it has many advantages. You don't have to do any of the maintenance. You can live in the best part of any city instead of way out in the suburbs. You have more flexibility to move for work.

People should always rent until they have children. If you don't know for certain that you'll be staying in one place for ten years, it's not worth it to buy a house for personal use.

It's much better to use your money to invest in something when you're at that age. If you can buy a house, buy it as a rental. If you can start a company, do that. A house that you live in gives you no return on your investment. It'll gradually appreciate in value, but at nowhere near the rate of return you can get from doing just about anything else.

But it depends on where you want to live and what kind of life you want to have. Look at me. I rent right now. I'm single, so it makes sense, but even if I were married, I would still rent.

Even if I had a child, I would still rent because I want to live in the best city with the best restaurants. That's the life I want, and I can rent where I want to live for a fraction of the cost of buying.

Another major advantage of renting is that it allows you to go after opportunities all over the world. You are not locked down in one city. You can go anywhere and do anything. This may be the biggest benefit of renting that no one ever talks about.

The house I bought in my twenties? I got more out of it when I turned it into a rental. When I was starting out in real estate, I kept buying houses for my own use. I turned every one of them into a rental. You don't want to tie down your capital. Every house you buy should be a flip or an investment property. Your plan should always be to refinance the down payment back out. It's an investment that will generate cash flow through rental or you want to sell it at profit within a year.

The biggest destruction of young people's wealth is making down payments for new houses. It is totally unnecessary, and I feel bad for the people who've been misled into tying their whole future to a single piece of property. There's a whole industry out there, a whole culture to convince people that home ownership is the key to financial security.

But do you really want that house? Do you need it? Maybe you really don't. A house is a never-ending parade of projects and repairs. It's a life sentence in the suburbs to live out the rat race like everybody else.

The reality of the New Rich is renting. When you have the cash flow mind-set, you think about what you really want and what it'll cost you. You want to live downtown in the best neighborhoods? You rent. I've bought lots of houses in my life. Sometimes I lived in them. But guess what? The places I've really wanted to live have always been rentals.

Once you have your cash flow established, you can buy if you want to. I probably will buy a house to live in when I get married and have children, but I'll be able to get the house I really want, not the one I could afford to make a down payment on when I was twenty-something. I'll also pay cash for it because I have so much passive income coming in.

Between interest on your mortgage, taxes, repairs, and everything else, buying a house is a worse deal than renting nine times out of ten. It ties up your savings and income for years and years.

Real estate, however, really is the ideal asset class. It's just that you need to treat it as an active investment and not as a retirement plan. Real estate is a much better place to invest than where most people put their money.

Ninety-nine percent of people invest in the stock market. They invest in readily available financial products that don't take much brain power. Stocks, bonds, mutual funds. They put it in a 401(k), which is also the stock market, but if 99% of people are all investing in the stock market, do you really think it's going to have the best returns?

Of course not. It doesn't make sense. If 99% of people are doing it, then how does that make sense?

People think it's too late to get into real estate or start a business. That couldn't be further from the truth. That's what 1% of people are doing with their money. That's where the opportunities for returns really are.

I have money in the stock market, but I think it's my riskiest investment. If the stock market performs exactly how you want it to, you're probably looking at a 7% annual yield for ten years, but that's not taking into account the huge downside risks and taxes you will pay on that 7%. Look at all the mini-crashes we have every year, all the time. The market is way, way down. I'm making money right now because my real estate is making money. The stock market is a joke. It's hardly better than a checking account.

Real estate generally makes between 20% and 60% in the first year, and it can be much, much more. People don't want to tell you this. It's crazy. You can hardly even imagine, but your money will double every two years if you invest in real estate and refinance that real estate.

The moment you refinance it becomes infinite. You could buy a subpar property and still make 20% return annually. Compared with 7% for stocks, that's barely making money, and if you have half a brain, you should be able to make much more than that with real estate. You really have to screw the pooch to be pulling in only 20%.

Options open up, too, when you've secured your cash flow from real estate. I invest in companies. You can get insane returns on these investments—from 100% to infinite—but those opportunities are only available to 1% of the people. You only get in on the ground floor when you know the right people, and you need to have the cash on hand to seize those opportunities.

The more you get into business investment, the higher your profile and the less risky it becomes. If you know what you're doing, it becomes far less risky than investing in the stock market. In the soft market, you have no control over the company. Just because it's making a profit doesn't mean its stock will go up.

It's like *Shark Tank*. The sharks are more than willing to throw $50K at someone with a good idea because they know that their help and their management oversight will allow them to make an infinite return on that $50K. That's much less risky than the stock market, and I'm in the same boat. It's the perfect example of American capitalism and leverage at work.

Real estate and becoming a credit investor will change your life. Even if you're not an accredited investor, you'll have opportunities that most people never even dream of. They talk about the rich getting richer. This is how they do it. That's what comes when you get good at business.

That's why it's so critical to get started now. If you get good at rental real estate or business, you can start putting money into opportunities with minimal time on your part. Your returns will be so vast. It will make the stock market look like a joke.

The investment tools that most people rely on are a joke. The 401(k) is a joke. It's good that it helps you out a little bit with your taxes, but you can't use that money. That's part of the game. If you use a 401(k), you're being gamed.

Once I was in the zero tax bracket due to real estate, I withdrew all my money from my 401(k). I could use that money, and if I invested it in real estate, I didn't have to pay any taxes anyway. The money in a 401(k) is locked up until you're 62. It's highway robbery, but it's all part of the system.

It's the system to keep you employed in the paycheck mindset. It's taking your money and locking it up so that you can't leave your job for decades. You avoid paying taxes on the money you put in, but then you get taxed at your income level on the way out. The 401(k) is a big part of the American Hoax. The more people invest in it, the more they need to stay. It's all part of the game.

If you invest in real estate, you don't need a 401(k). You can use that money to do what you want. Grow your assets, increase your cash flow. Or just go on that trip you've always wanted to. Eat a nice meal out whenever you want.

The tax savings of the 401(k) will also look like a pittance when compared with the tax advantages of real estate as an asset class. Rental real estate investing is a far superior tax-deferred account than a 401(k). If you invest in real estate, you never need a 401(k).

Chapter 8

Taxes and Administration

There are significant tax advantages to real estate when compared with other assets. Compared with earning a paycheck and paying income tax, it's a completely different ball game. Minimizing your tax bill is the key to making the cash flow lifestyle pay for your wildest dreams. Taking advantage of the tax breaks associated with real estate is the easiest, quickest way to retire young and start living the good life.

I am not a tax professional. Everyone reading this book should consult a tax professional when investing in real estate. A tax professional is absolutely essential to help you understand and follow the law, while helping you minimize your tax burden through legal means. Tax professionals do not find loopholes in the tax code or abet their clients in defrauding the government. They help you understand policies and provisions that exist to spur the kind of investment we're talking about.

It's also essential that you are classified as a real estate professional for tax purposes. This is something your accountant can help you with, but you'll need to get this classification once your portfolio has reached a certain size. This is another reason why it's essential to work with a tax professional if you want to make money in real estate. The most important reason to be classified as a real estate professional is for tax purposes. To write off more than $25K in real estate losses, you must qualify as a real estate professional for that tax year.

Understanding taxes will allow you to become more successful than the most powerful CEO at your company, just from renting real estate. This chapter details my experience using tax advantages to grow my assets, with the collaboration of various tax professionals.

I started out by buying one rental property at a time. My sweet spot was acquiring houses at $80K that needed $10K to $15K in repairs and would then rent for $1,000 to $1,500 a month. I would be all in on the deal at $95K. When it was time to refinance the property, it would appraise for $130K to $135K like clockwork. This means that if I got an 80% loan-to-value loan on my refinance, I would be able to pull $104K worth of debt on the property. At closing, we take the $104K loan and pay off the original loan at $95K. All in all, I walk away with roughly $5K tax-free cash at closing while still owning the asset and its cash flow.

So the house is more than free. It pays you to own it. If you can do this, you can buy an unlimited number of rental properties.

You can find a property like that anywhere in the United States. If you live in an expensive city, $100K might only get you a modest house, but maybe an hour away you'll find a smaller city where you can get something like this.

So you have the $100,000 property and you're making $500 a month cash flow. That may not seem like much, but you end up making $6,000 a year tax free after all expenses and mortgage payments have been paid. That may not seem like a lot. You're thinking to yourself that you would need to own ten houses like that to make $60,000 a year? Or twenty houses to break $100,000?

But you're not thinking about the value of tax-free cash flow, and that's what rental income is all about. At the same time you're paying off the mortgage, the property is appreciating in value. Making $6,000 a year tax free is really like making $12,000 a year. Every dollar you make renting real estate is worth two dollars you'd make in corporate America.

At the same time, you offset other sources of income. Your profit is $6,000, your cash flow is $6,000, but you're going to be able to write of $12,000 if you segregate depreciation.

Segregating depreciation is a powerful tool in minimizing your tax liability. In a nutshell, normal depreciation for a multifamily investment is based on 27.5 years. If you segregate depreciation, you accelerate your depreciation in the first five to ten years by allowing you to take roughly double the amount of depreciation. Please consult your accountant for the specific numbers and calculations, but this should absolutely be part of your tax strategy.

All this combines to create significant tax advantages. If you're still working your corporate job, your taxes for that income are going to go down. Talk about powerful! Not only is your cash flow tax free, but your income from other sources also becomes more tax efficient when you segregate depreciation.

Now, as you can imagine, if you do that ten times, you'll never have to work again in your life. A $100,000 property is so much more to you than just the rental income. Each house acquisition gives you roughly a $3,000 a year raise in your corporate job through tax savings..

Now imagine that you buy a $1 million apartment building. Everything scales up. Right away that's roughtly $40,000 annually in tax-free cash flow, which is basically the equivalent of earning a $80,000 salary when you consider it is all tax free. Most people can live off of that, especially if you don't get caught up with buying the bigger house or the faster car every couple of years. You could dive right in and get a $1 million apartment building and never work again a day in your life.

Someone who's thirty-three years old or has maybe $100,000 saved could quit their job, withdraw the money from their 401(k), buy a $1 million apartment building, and never work again. You could scale that by adding value, refinancing, and using 1031 exchanges when moving up to bigger properties. The process can be repeated for continual growth for the rest of your life.

But it's probably better to start with houses. Start with a single house to rent. That'll show you the effects on both cash flow and your tax return. You'll see how it works in miniature, and it'll teach you everything you need to know to scale it up.

This isn't a loophole. This is the way taxes work throughout the world. Depreciation is the same everywhere, and there's a reason for this. It incentivizes investors to build and maintain housing. Things would fall into disrepair. You wouldn't have the shining cities and leafy neighborhoods we have here, and every other country in the world knows this.

You can read the IRS tax code, and it will tell you the best places to invest your money. Real estate has the longest history of providing these benefits, but every year there's something new. It could be drilling for oil. Or building the next Facebook. If society needs something, the government puts tax savings investments in the tax code so that people will invest in it. It's like the opposite of the cigarette tax. They don't want people to smoke, so they jack up the tax on cigarettes.

It's the same idea with real estate. We want really good real estate that increases in value. The tax code allows investors some of the best tax advantages on the planet to maintain our housing and real estate industries because it's in society's interest to have high-quality real estate.

Aside from the cash flow, the main reason to invest in real estate is the tax advantages. I cannot stress this enough. Taxes matter. You always have to remember: it's not how much you make. It's how much you keep. Real estate lowers your tax liability for any other income, and if you give up your job completely, then everything is tax free.

I'm at a $10 million investment level, so the tax write-offs are significant. They're in the hundreds of thousands of dollars. Almost millions. I pay no taxes on other businesses that I own because of the real estate.

They released one of Donald Trump's tax returns, and it was negative $900 million. This is someone working at the billion-dollar real estate level, and he doesn't have to pay taxes for an entire decade.

When you refinance and pull that equity out, that's also tax free. You do not pay tax on increasing your loan. So this gives you a big surge of money that's not taxed, which you can use to buy more investment properties. Then if you sell your houses and roll that money into apartment buildings as I did, you can do that transaction so that the profit and depreciation carry into the next building. That's the 1031 exchange. Your income is tax free. Every time you refinance and pile on more debt is tax free. It's ridiculous. You can pay almost nothing in taxes in real estate forever.

When you're investing at this level, the money is going to multiply quicker than you ever thought possible. That's because of the tax-free nature of this investment. Refinancing, investing in bigger and bigger properties. If I were taxed at each of these steps, it would not have been possible to grow my portfolio as quickly as I did. I will keep doing this my entire life and never pay taxes until the very end. By then, I'll have so much money that the tax liability will be nothing. I'll also be ninety, and then I'll die, so it won't matter anyway.

You have to think about the time value of money. Money is worth more now. You use the money now to buy bigger properties, which will make you more money in the future. You push your tax liability back to the point where it won't even matter, and you're set for life.

There's another tax trick that I've used my entire career. Let me give you an example. Say you bought an $80,000 property and financed the repairs to the tune of $15,000. You got a loan for $95,000 to cover those costs, including the repairs. Immediately, that year, you can write off the entire $15,000 you put into repairs against other income and against cash flow. Make sure you do this in conjunction with your accountant. So what just happened?

You got a loan from the bank for the $15K in repairs, making your net loan proceeds $95K for acquisitions plus repairs. The $15K is part of the loan, so you didn't really spend $15K of your own money, but you can write off $15K that same year as repair expenses! Again, you must check with your accountant, but that is a major advantage! Get a few houses, and scale that up. Pretty soon you will be in a negative tax position and may never pay taxes again. True!

That's why you need to add value. If you add value, you can refinance your money out quicker and write off the expenses if you include them in the loan. That's how Donald Trump was able to write off negative $900 million in the '90s. He had billions of dollars of loans and repairs included in those loans. He was able to take a repair expense deduction on most of those repair costs that same year even though he really didn't pay out of pocket for those expenses. That's what I call powerful.

That's in addition to the write-offs for depreciation. It puts you in a negative tax position that can help you minimize your corporate income tax or anything else. Shortly after I started doing real estate full-time, I started my private label company on the side. I was selling supplements and skin care products, and the real estate helped minimize taxes related to my businesses. I sold one of my companies for a decent amount of money and was able to avoid paying capital gain taxes on the sale due to my negative tax position from my real estate. Real estate is so much more than just a source of cash flow. It helps you minimize your taxes in all other areas of your life as well.

This is why it's important to have a good accountant. If you want to make it in the cash flow mind-set, you're going to need a good accountant, who will know everything I'm talking about and more. Even if you have only one rental property, you need a professional accountant.

You also have to do your homework. Many accountants don't want to segregate depreciation because it's more work for them. It should just happen automatically. So you need to know about the tax advantages available to you and challenge your accountant to get what you want.

The tax savings are so incredible in real estate that the IRS is going to take a closer look at you. You need an accountant to do your taxes so that everything is by the book. I had four properties before I realized I needed an accountant. I was doing all my taxes on my own, and I wasn't getting the most out of my investment. So I found an accountant who specialized in real estate, and everything went much better for me.

Don't just accept what your accountant says as the endgame. You need to have some idea what you're talking about so that you can challenge him. Make him do the work for you. Your money is worth it, and he'll do what you say up to the point where he loses his license. It won't come to that, though, because the major tax advantages of real estate are all nice and legal.

An accountant can be expensive, but it's worth it for a good one. It will pay off for you in the long run if you can find someone who knows what's what and who takes care of your interests.

It's funny. You meet some people, such as accountants or bankers, who are supposed to know everything about how money works, but they don't even own an apartment building themselves. You would think that all these professionals who will lend you money would know something about making money, but they actually don't. You'd think that a banker willing to lend you a million dollars would know something about rental properties. Apparently not because they don't own any.

I've found that more accountants own rental properties than bankers because they know the tax advantages. They've done their clients' taxes. They've seen the power of real estate. Find an accountant who invests in real estate himself. That'll be a good indicator.

Real estate agents or other investors can also put you in touch with a good accountant, but you have to know the tax advantages yourself to push them to do good work for you. Sometimes the accountant wants the easy way out and won't do the work. You have to know about it to ask for it.

The tax advantages of real estate are one of the best reasons to invest in this asset class. You'll be generating tax-free cash flow through rentals that will offset other income through segregated depreciation. For your entire life, you can sell in and out of real estate tax free. You can buy up. Every time you refinance an investment out, that's also tax free. If you continue the whole process, you can become a multimillionaire.

So go buy more property!

Chapter 9

Passion Projects and the Essential Side Hustle

The best way to approach the quit your job concept is to have a plan. I'm not telling you to quit your job without a plan. That's suicide. You need some money to get started, and you need a plan to sustain yourself.

It also helps to learn how to work—to see how other people build things that make money. It's nice to say that you can just start out as an entrepreneur, but the reality is that we all need money to start, and we need experience of one kind or another.

So it's not the worst thing in the world to start working in corporate America.

Working in corporate America can be a good experience if you're getting the right things out of it. The trick is that you can't let your experience be defined by your employment. Don't just accept everything they tell you at face value. Look at how things actually work. Not even from the perspective of your manager or your manager's manager. See how it works for the owners. See how it works as a business. If you work for a company that's even halfway decent, you'll learn a lot that you can apply to your own projects.

There is value to starting in corporate America. You might be able to start companies right out of college, but that's hard, and you will struggle to have the start-up capital you really need. Aside from the circumstances of my departure, my job in corporate America was ultimately a positive experience.

That company was great, and I was leading one of the best lives possible in corporate America. It wasn't the same as being financially free, but I don't see how else I could have really gotten started.

But I know people who did it differently. You can make start-up money tending bar and have no background doing any formal business endeavor. The important thing is to have some sort of stabilizing income while you work on the side.

That's how I approached it. After three years working in corporate America, I started buying houses. One house a year to build up my portfolio, and I invested in real estate on the side.

I was able to retire when this work became full-time, and real estate has the advantage of giving you so much free time that you can spend pursuing other work or passion projects.

A passion project is anything you do that you do primarily for yourself. It won't necessarily make you money, but it matters to you. See the world, save the rain forest, play in a band. It's whatever gets you up in the morning.

Working on the side is more like an experiment in cash flow. It's trying something that will make you money. It might not be a lot of money at first. You might find that you can't make money with it at all, but the right work can make you more money than you ever imagined possible.

After I quit my corporate job, my main work was real estate investing. The advantage of such work was that it didn't take a lot of my time, so I could develop new work on the side. My first work was selling supplements and skin care products online. One of my real estate partners did this full-time, so I started out working for him. It was just for fun, really. I didn't need the money, but I was excited about it. He taught me the ropes, and pretty soon I was making good money.

It's obvious that selling online is the easiest way to make money in the Internet Age. I love real estate. It's both my passion and my primary source of income, but why not also sell something online? It's the way of the future.

Once I was learning how online sales worked, I started developing other projects. I got into private labeling. I built something up, but I went incredibly slowly. I didn't have the desperation of it being my main or only work. Real estate gave me the security to grow at the right pace. When the time was right, I started my own company, and now my new sideline is selling supplements online.

Then the two businesses start to benefit each other. I take the profits I make selling supplements online and invest them into real estate. The tax advantages of real estate make my supplements business that much more tax efficient.

Writing this book is a side-hustle. It's also something I'm passionate about. Reading books helped me become the entrepreneur I am today. I want people to read this book and know that it's possible.

When you find success, your side-hustle becomes your main hustle. Then you find a new side-hustle. It's an ongoing process. I'll always have something on the go from now on. Or maybe everything I do is a side-hustle because I don't really have to work anymore.

The importance of working on the side is having something next in line. You're going to have so much time on your hands once you quit your job. It's easy to let that time go to waste. It's better to take on all the things you've ever dreamed of. Your passions and your ideas to make money. Anything you've ever wanted to do.

I always wanted to travel the world, but you can't really do that when you have a corporate job, and you can only take off a couple of weeks a year.

So I backpacked in Southeast Asia for two months by myself, which was incredible. I was staying at hostels. I was meeting people from all over the world. I went to five different countries in two months. Tell me who can do that in corporate America. You can be the CEO, the big kahuna, and you'll never have time to indulge in something like that.

Then I travelled a month in Europe. Now I'm planning to do two or three months in South America. There's a whole world to explore, and that's just the travel aspect. But that's a big deal in itself because nothing will make you grow more than traveling the world.

I've never met a successful person who hasn't travelled the world. By the same token, I've never met a successful person who works in corporate America because the two things are mutually exclusive. The two weeks of vacation you get in a corporate job do not allow for real traveling.

A typical vacation for someone in corporate America consists of going down to Cancun for a week while you abuse your body with alcohol and unhealthy food, only to come home feeling very unhealthy. That's not fulfilling travel. Real travel happens when you opt-out of the resort option, and instead immerse yourself in real culture.

If that is your ideal vacation, then try this instead. Cancel your binge drinking trip to Cancun, and come down to Florida's beaches (which are better), drink coffee, attend a real estate investing seminar, and read a book. That is a trip that will pay you dividends long after the trip is over.

Travel can be something you do on the side. It can be more than just having a good time. Maybe you want to help hungry children in Africa. Maybe you want to volunteer at a nature preserve. These might be more like passion projects. You probably won't make any money doing such things, but you might build something. You could put in the time to build an NGO that does real good in the world.

But you can't change the world like that if you're putting all your time into working for someone else. A corporate job will consume your life. It will eat up the time you could be putting to better use.

It's funny, but in my experience, working on the side has always ended up making me more money than my main interest. Real estate made me more than I ever made in corporate America just one year after I quit. In the past year, supplements made me more cash than real estate for the first time. They're actually very close right now, but your side work can become your main objective. Then you need something else that may become the next main thing. It's kind of crazy.

My private label companies are making more money than my real estate at this point, and it was something I did on the side. This book is an example. I don't plan to make money on it. It's mostly a passion project. Just something to help people see the truth about what's really going on and if I help just one person achieve financial freedom with this book, then it will be a complete success.

That's the ethos of working on the side. Before you quit your job, start investing in real estate—not just as an end in itself but to bridge you to something more. Then start doing something on the side with the time and money you now have. Start selling something online. Follow your passions. Find the money.

But be smart about it. Let me make this easy: you should start selling online. Get a real estate portfolio for the cash flow and tax advantages, but then you should focus on online sales because the reality is that it's never been easier to make money.

You can make money with just about any idea because the Internet gives you access to all these niches. You don't need the next big idea. All I did was sell supplements with my own label that other people were selling, and I made a million dollars doing that.

There are so many people in the world, and they're now all connected. The Internet is the easiest sales platform ever invented. Don't waste money opening a storefront when you can sell online. You can sell anything online and make a million dollars.

Here's the big secret. You need to find the niche. The money is in the niches. You can sell virtually any product, something that is functionally the same as anybody else's product, but if you can appeal to a niche, you're going to make money. That's why selling online is best.

Even if you want to do something else, you need to advertise online. That's where all the eyeballs are every hour of every day. You have to be online one way or another to make money today.

But it's such a great opportunity, and it's never been easier. I hate to say this, but in some ways it's even easier than real estate. The learning curve to sell online is a little bit steeper, but it's nothing incredible.

Maybe I'm just caught up in the excitement of it all. The energy of such work taking off is infectious, but it's better to start in real estate, which is still my passion and always will be. It's unparalleled for cash flow and tax advantages.

That's the beauty of working on the side. You're not stuck doing one thing for the rest of your life as you are in corporate America. There will always be a new challenge, a new opportunity, and real estate will give you the time and capital to pursue other interests and passions.

There's a world of opportunity out there, and it will be yours to explore.

Conclusion

The Road Less Traveled

Travel is important to me. Many people want to travel, but they think you have to be rich to do it. That's not true. Anybody can travel. The trick is that you have to think about travel with the cash flow mind-set.

When I went to Southeast Asia, I had just sold my houses, and I was getting into apartment buildings. I was living in one of the houses I'd just sold, so I timed it in a way that I didn't have to pay any rent. It was the perfect opportunity for me to go to Southeast Asia.

Traveling by yourself really opens up your mind to the world. You experience a new culture. You see people and sites completely different from what you grew up with, and because I wasn't paying any rent, I actually saved money by traveling. You do not need to be rich to travel the world if you understand your cash flow.

It also depends on how you travel. If you go to an all-inclusive resort, you're going to pay more, which is the same with a cruise, but do you really want some curated experience where everything is laid out for you? If that's what you want, you might as well stay in your corporate job. If what you want is freedom and adventure, you can travel anywhere and spend much less money.

If you stay in hostels or cheaper hotels, it actually comes out cheaper than what you pay in rent in the United States. I'm not talking about dives infested with all kinds of crawling things. There are nice places that are just ever so slightly off the beaten path. I saved money by traveling the world.

I could also travel without interrupting my cash flow. With the Internet, you can be connected to your business from anywhere in the world. I could work for an hour in the morning and take care of everything with my real estate and supplements businesses. On some days, I wouldn't even have to turn on the computer. I'd just make sure everything was all right. That's the beauty of passive income businesses.

Think of the leverage that gives you. You can own and operate companies today and travel the world at the same time—all because you have a computer and you're connected to the Internet. That's leverage.

Why spend your days driving an hour each way to get to work? Why tie yourself down to a house in the suburbs? To a city you don't want to live in? Why waste your life on a corporate job just to give away half of what you make in taxes?

I'm talking about true freedom. I never felt more free in my life than when I went to Southeast Asia while still making money. I felt more powerful at that time than at any other point in my life.

What everyone needs to understand is that their goal should be to become financially free, not to become a millionaire. I know quite a few millionares who still work a 9-5. In reality, if they were successful, they wouldn't need a job, but because they don't have the right mindset, they continue to "need" their job.

Your goal should not be to live out the American Dream. If your goal isn't freedom, then what are you doing here?

Money rules the world whether you like it or not. Our government is based on capitalism. Everything revolves around money. If you're the type of person who says you don't want to be rich or don't want to make money, then what do you want out of life? Why would you not want to make money? It makes everything so much easier.

My goal in this book is to tell you that there are other ways to make money. Maybe the rat race is driving you insane and you fantasize about quitting everything. Well, quit that corporate job, but have a plan to make money in a way that will make you financially free.

If you don't make it huge now, you're going to wind up just like everybody else. You're not going to be able to change the world. You're going to be just the same as everyone else. You don't want to be that. If that's what you want, then you might as well just give up, but there's more to life than that.

Anybody can invest in real estate. There's a shortage of people investing in real estate. Again, 1% of people own and operate companies and invest in real estate. Ninety-nine percent of people work in corporate America. Who will make more money? It's easier to make money when you're only going up against 1% of the people.

To drive society, our American education system was built to develop employees and rightfully so. Not everyone can be an entrepreneur because we wouldn't actually be successful as a species if that were the case.

But I wish they had a curriculum for the real estate investor. I wish an option existed where you could learn how to be an entrepreneur even when you are a high school student because so many important skills are just not taught in schools. Many people would benefit if that were at least an option. I know I would have eaten that up.

But it means that there are lots of opportunities out there—opportunities for everybody. If you want to change your life, real estate is the quickest way to retire. You can retire with a net worth of zero and be set up for the rest of your life.

The Internet is the quickest way to make millions of dollars today. Everybody is connected. There's a whole new world of connections out there. Get out and find your niche.

The main takeaway from this book is that you've been sold a pack of lies. The American Dream is the American Hoax. Everything you learned in school was just to teach you to be an employee. A modern-day slave. If you want to be like everybody else, there's nothing for you in this book. You might as well stop reading.

If you made it this far, however, then you're starting to wake up. You're starting to see that the corporate world can offer you no progression. You're starting to wonder how you can organize your life around the goal of financial freedom.

I have seven years of experience in corporate America as a modern-day slave, and I have three years of experience as an entrepreneur. My net worth has increased by twenty times ever since I quit my job. My life has become something out of a movie.

I live in an amazing city: St. Petersburg, Florida. I golf four times a week, and I can do whatever I want, whenever I want.

There were serious learning pains. You are going against the grain if you choose this life, and many people will make it tough for you—people who will fuel your doubts and call you crazy because they completely buy into the American Dream, and what you're doing could puncture their whole reality.

But I'm telling you that it's going to be rewarding. Financially rewarding, personally rewarding. God only knows what I'll accomplish by the time I'm forty. Maybe my next work will turn into the next big thing. Who can say? But I'm out there, and I'm trying. My job now is just to own and operate all types of companies. I'm almost like a shark.

If you want a life like everybody else's, then work in corporate America. If you want to live the life that everyone deserves, you need to immediately start investing in real estate but also doing something on the side.

I know you want to be financially free. Would you rather be a slave? That's insanity. Money rules the world. Money makes everything better.

It's time to take control of your life, escape the great American Hoax, and LIVE FREE!

Thanks so much for reading my book. I truly appreciate you taking the time to hear my story. I was shy to release it at first, but it got to the point where I felt that I needed to share my story, so I said fuck it and released it.

As a small time author, reviews are important to me. I personally read every review, and take the comments to heart as I think about the next edition, as well as with the other projects I'm working on.

Before you go out there and become a millionaire, I would be grateful for a nice review.

To your success, **Oliver**.

Made in the USA
San Bernardino, CA
07 May 2020

70800718R00058